EFFICIENT STAFF TRAINING

EFFICIENT STAFF TRAINING

By

William G. Fern

MAXFORD BOOKS

New Delhi (INDIA)

EFFICIENT STAFF TRAINING

Reprint : 2016
First Published 2009

ISBN : 81-8116-075-4

Published by :
MAXFORD BOOKS
Sales Office: 4264/3, IInd Floor, Ansari Road,
Darya Ganj, New Delhi-110 002
Ph.: 011-65156284
Regd. Office: 95, Medha Apartments, Mayur Vihar,
Phase-I, Delhi-110 091
Ph.: 011-22743537
E-mail: maxfordbooks@hotmail.com

Printed at: Ashim Printline, Delhi-92

CONTENTS

INTRODUCTION

AS my time is more and more taken up by personal staff training and business organising, it becomes apparent that it will be impossible for me to accept all the engagements offered, as I am occupied for months ahead as business counsel to an increasing number of firms.

I am now writing over a hundred reports a year, and as this work is increasing I am placing before my readers the methods I have used since I came to this country from South Africa, in organising businesses, so that others may take advantage of these successful methods.

This book is not only interesting reading but is a textbook for any alert executive to use in training his staff.

The methods used in forming Service Clubs are fully explained, and also how they can be operated.

I have included many of the successful lectures I recommend for all sections of a staff.

I have myself been astonished at the extra-ordinary results obtained.

One firm has increased sales 100% in two years.

Another 60%.

Another (a very large firm, one of the leaders) 55%.

The lowest figure recorded is 18% increase, while one business reports a nearly trebled increase since I first started staff training with them.

These facts make the demand for such a book as this, so it is published in the hope that these methods can be carried on, improved, enlarged and expanded by those who believe there is a way to "Get more Fun out of the Job."

WILLIAM G. FERN.

CHAPTER ONE

HOW TO ORGANISE A STAFF FOR GREATER EFFICIENCY

NOT more than 500 firms in Britain have availed themselves of the new note in business organising.

It is generally known as Staff Training, and its purpose is to train the Staff both individually and in the mass.

The larger the business becomes, the more difficult it is for the principal executives to spread their personality and influence through to all members of the staff.

The methods described in this book can be used for a staff of six, or six hundred, although in the latter case it would be more economical to call in the aid of an outside expert.

To the executive who is courageous enough to try this plan, he will find, as a result, that a new spirit and a new enthusiasm is awakened in his organisation.

These are the advantages of staff training:

1. You build the team spirit.
2. You lessen errors.
3. You lessen labour turnover.
4. You will not have to go outside for men to promote.
5. You lower costs.
6. You increase the business.
7. You obtain a steady flow of valuable suggestions of great use to the firm.
8. The oldest business is brought up-to-date.
9. The staff becomes happier.
10. The latent ability of the staff is developed.
11. You begin to put the Saturday afternoon spirit into the Monday morning job.
12. The Directors get as much benefit as anyone.

It needs a courageous executive to determine to carry out the ideas of this book, and you can start staff training in a month.

WHAT TO DO FIRST

Get together (if your staff is large enough) twelve of your most enthusiastic executives and tell them you wish to establish a Service Club.

Use whatever points are necessary from this book at this committee meeting, and arrange a general meeting of all members of the staff.

Use the lectures for a basis of a talk every fortnight on the lines of the agenda on page 16.

In five or six months the meetings will have become so much a part of the organisation that subjects for the agenda for future meetings will flow in.

A WORD OF CAUTION

Be prepared for the fact that, at the beginning few will be interested—that will come once the staff understand you have established what is essential, a Parliament in their midst.

Be prepared to stick. There will be much that will discourage you, but determine to carry on, and gradually the fervour and enthusiasm you have aroused will carry the movement onward and upward to the higher ideals of modern business.

LEADERSHIP NECESSARY

From my experience, it is essential that the chief or chiefs of any organisation take an active part in this movement.

If the organisation and conduct of the Club is left to a subordinate that is as high as the spirit of enthusiasm will rise.

Just as water cannot rise any higher than its source, so is it true in staff training that you can only expect these splendid results already obtained when the chief executive throws his heart and soul into it.

Personally, in my work I refuse to go on when I find the chiefs are not interested. It is absolutely essential that the man at the top is at the top, as chairman, at least.

Of course, he may not conduct the meetings, although he should, but at least he must be present at every meeting and say a word or two—be it ever so few.

So remember the first rule—*the man at the top*—or don't commence.

Another advantage of this movement is the inflow of new ideas.

I have never yet gone into a business with-out seeing at the end of six months at least 100 new ideas in operation.

In the last business I was in four new suggestions were in operation the day following my visit.

This is another reason why this movement needs the man at the top to shepherd it.

HOW TO ORGANISE A SERVICE CLUB IN YOUR FIRM

1. Issue an invitation to all members of the staff to be present at the first meeting.
2. Provide a little refreshment, if possible.
3. This meeting to be addressed by a Director, the Chairman to be present, and the Managing Director.
4. Rules. A general set of rules are attached. You can adapt these rules as you wish.
5. Officers. The important officers of the Club are the Chairman and the Secretary. Choose these officers with care. The former is responsible for the conduct of the meetings and must be enthusiastic and capable of leadership. You may need an Attendance Officer and a Programme Officer.
6. The Chairman. Please inspire your Club to act as an example to the rest of the members of the firm who may not be members. You owe a responsibility and duty to those who, like you are banded together in these Clubs, to develop a higher standard of personal and business efficiency. All eyes are on you. Justify the closest scrutiny.

HOW TO CONDUCT THE MEETINGS

In order to ensure the success of the meetings, it is important that the Chairman adheres closely to the Agenda.

If discussion ensues, and it is likely to be lengthy, ask for a definite resolution, secure a seconder, and then have the matter inserted in the minutes so that it can be confirmed at the subsequent meeting.

If the Chairman is in doubt, it is better to ask for notice of motion, and have the matter fully debated at the next meeting. Such notice of motion must appear on the Agenda for the following meeting.

If there is ever a falling off of attendance, appoint members of the Club to interview the absent members and "re-sell" the Club to them.

You should , have a fortnightly meeting. Some firms have monthly meetings.

Agendas should be compiled for twelve meetings, or six at least.

AGENDAS

The following suggestions for the Agenda for meetings are offered after sixteen years' experience of such Clubs:—

The meeting should be timed to last one hour. Run your meeting to time.

The Agendas are organised to give:

1. Two quarters of an hour to ten-minute papers, and discussion by members.

2. One quarter of an hour, to discussion on one of the Chapter's series of test questions.

3. One quarter of an hour, to a demonstration sale, if the Club is at all interested in selling.

   OR

4. One quarter of an hour, to an analysis of the Chapter the Club is studying at the time.

This makes up the hour.

If you have a large number of members, split the series of test questions up among them.

If a six-fold membership, then one member can give a review of the whole of the questions. If a twelve-fold membership, then divide up the questions. If a twenty-five-fold member-ship, then call for volunteers, or appoint members to discuss one question only, and so cover the whole series of questions.

This refers to "2" above.

Here is a regular agenda, presuming that the meeting commences at 6 p.m.:—

6.00 Minutes.

6.02 10-Minute Paper.

6.12 Discussion.

6.15 10-Minute Paper.

6.25 Discussion.

6.30 Demonstration Sale Criticism. OR

Paper on Chapter No.

Followed by Discussion.

6.45 Analysis of Test Questions:

By 1

2

3

4

5

Adjournment, after arranging next meeting.

FIFTY SUBJECTS FOR PAPERS AND DISCUSSIONS

1.—Standards in our business.

2.—Records that save labour.

3.—How time is wasted.

4.—Psychology and what it means to me.

5.—Better letters.

6.—The value of analysis.

7.—Handling men.

8.—Concentration.

9.—Optimism.

10.—Our advertising.

11.—Courage as an asset.

12.—Ambition : Is it dangerous ?

13.—Is service worth while?

14.—The power of will.

15.—The best way to approach new clients.

16.—How to close a sale.

17.—Errors, their cause and cure.

18.—Personality and its cultivation.

19.—The team spirit.

20.—Time values.

21.—Determination, and what it accomplishes.

22.—The history of the firm.

23.—Every job important, and why.

24.—The fun in the job.

25.—Acting with tact.

26.—Plans that save time.

27.—Graph charts I know.

28.—Wasted effort, its cause and cure.

29.—Character Analysis.

30.—Public Speaking.

31.—How to keep fit.

32.—How the mind works.

33.—Enthusiasm.

34.—Loyalty.

35.—Faith.

36.—Is the customer always right?

37.—Courtesy in business.

38.—Why do some men get on?

39.—The value of a good memory.

40.—How to analyse the selling territory.

41.—Studying the customer.

42.—Telephone, and its value to us.

43.—Selling it by letter.

44.—Happiness, in spite of—

45.—Efficiency reward, for employer and employee.

46.—Success as I understand it.

47.—The Manager's job.

48.—The romance of business.

49.—Getting on in the world.

50.—The greatest asset in business.

Additional titles of subjects sent on request.

OBJECTS OF THE CLUB

1. To study Personal Efficiency, Self-Management, Management in its Scientific aspect, to study Psychology and to apply it to the individual, the home, the vocation and to the community.

2. To study service, and to endeavour faith-fully to apply the principles daily.

3. To promote better business methods, and to encourage my fellow members towards the attainments of 100% efficiency.

4. To understand the principles of Scientific Management or Salesmanship, and to apply these principles to myself and for the benefit of my firm.

5. To study the philosophy of Action, and to adhere to the motto of all the Service Clubs that "Action is the only prayer that is answered."

RULES FOR "FERNFAX" BUSINESS SCIENCE AND SERVICE CLUBS

1. The name of the Club shall be "Service Club."

2. At the annual meeting members will vote and elect officers as follows : Chairman, Vice-Chairman and Secretary, if membership is less than fifteen; if over, elect three Committeemen, who shall perform the duties of Attendance Officer, Programme Convenor, Fraternal Officer. Additional officers may be elected according to the size of the Club. Such officers to hold office for one year. The Officers and Committee may elect any member to fill a vacancy that may arise.

3. The duties of the Attendance Officer shall be to be responsible for the attendance of all members, and to obtain reports for reason of absence. He shall report to the Chairman at each meeting.

4. The duties of the Programme Convenor shall be to secure members for the items of the Agendas, and to be sure that the full Agendas shall be worthily presented.

5. The Fraternal Officer shall see that all members know each other, and shall be responsible for any social development of the Club that may take place. In the small Clubs, the above three offices shall be filled by the Secretary.

6. Honorary members may be elected, if directors, or of other suitable executive standing.

7. Any of the above rules, or additional rules, may be altered or added to or deleted at a general meeting, after fourteen days' notice has been given and after two-thirds majority of those present vote in favour thereof.

HOW TO OBTAIN THE BEST RESULTS FROM THE FOLLOWING LECTURES

Read through the first lecture as though it were a novel.

Then re-read it, with a sheet of notepaper at hand.

Write down the headings of the important points.

Add to these points any special hint of application to your own business.

These outlines of the lecture should not take more than fifteen minutes to deliver.

If you are not accustomed to Public Speaking, you are advised to read Mr. Fern's book, "The Master Speaker."

The Publishers

CHAPTER TWO

GENERAL PRINCIPLES OF BUSINESS SCIENCE

IN order to succeed in business today, one learns the need of the study of its scientific principles in the same way as one would approach the study of law or medicine.

These principles are very definitely organised and, as you will observe, revolve around the Big Four in business:

1. You.
2. The User of what you sell, generally known as the Buyer.
3. The Idea, Service or Article sold, commonly known as the Goods.
4. The meeting of the minds of You and the Buyer in agreement, commonly known as the Sale.

In order to attain success in business, the latent power of the Big Four must be developed.

Most men, so psychologists say, are only 10% efficient, so far as the personal factor is concerned;

this book is designed to develop your latent power now within. In other words, you can look forward to a comfortable increase of your personal efficiency.

As the mind of the public changes, there must always be an ever-increasing desire to improve what you sell, and at least the desire to adapt it to the requirements of your users.

"Use your users," as the saying goes, and modern business relies on an ever-increasing market analysis of the customer's mind towards what is offered them for sale.

So that, when you sell a service, always more difficult to sell than goods, you study the service or the goods in terms of customer under-standing.

Psychology (the science of behaviour), as you will see from the next chapter, is being studied by business men in every country in its relation to selling.

Everybody in the world sells something.

A manager has to sell the ideal of the team spirit to the staff.

Every unit of the staff sells himself or her-self, by his or her work and behaviour, and the latter is often as important as the former.

The more the business man of today studies psychology, the quicker he will understand the eccentricities and idiosyncrasies of those with whom he wishes to attain mutual agreement.

So the Principles of Business Science revolve around these four factors :

1. You

2. The Buyer.

3. The Goods.

4. The Sale.

As I believe in taking readers into my confidence, I would like to tell you what this book aims at.

The objective is to interest you in yourself — in your deeper inner self—in the latent power within you, awaiting development, so that you can in turn arouse this latent power in the minds of your staff.

When you understand how you can increase your personal efficiency, you can then suggest to others how they can also apply some of these truths.

With a working knowledge of Efficiency, you can suggest improvements in your work, and, if in a position of authority, how others can improve too.

For you are one of the pioneers. Staff Training is so new that only a few chosen hundreds know anything about it.

It is a new evolving theme of scientific business, designed to co-ordinate the human element, and you will prepare yourself for that great work by first of all studying these basic principles, and then endeavouring to apply them.

What I ask you to do is to study each chapter carefully.

I always believe you should have a short synopsis in front of you, of each chapter, in case you wish to refer at any time to any of the studies in front of you.

The following is a brief synopsis of studies:

1. **GENERAL PRINCIPLES OF BUSINESS SCIENCE.**—The organised Principles of Business. Organised knowledge now available. The four divisions of Business. Principles of Finance. Principles of Administration. Principles of Distribution. Principles of Supply.

2. **PERSONAL PSYCHOLOGY.**—Self, Brains, Emotions, Will and the Body. To what extent is man master of his destiny? Twelve personality traits needed by the staff trainer.

3. **HOW THE MIND WORKS.**—The wonder of the mental machine. Why and how we think. Making brains grow. Judgment, the highest function of the mind. Deductive and inductive reasoning.

4. **THE MAGNETIC FORCE OF ENTHUSIASM.** —The ten secrets of business leadership. Courage, the golden thread of business. What faith means to

the business man. How to inspire loyalty. How to build the spirit.

5. MEMORY TRAINING. — The for and against of Systems. How to find your type of memory. Tests for eye memory, ear memory, and touch memory. Ten tips that improve memory.

6. EFFICIENCY PRINCIPLES.—The Emerson plan. Dr. Taylor. The late Frank Gilbreth. Practical application of principles. How to start evolution and not revolution.

7. STANDARDISED CONDITIONS AND OPERATIONS.— Why time is more important than money. How to get the staff to plan. Saving time each day. How to save time every week. Plans for the year. Planning for ten years. The importance of the big vision.

8. SALES PSYCHOLOGY. — Analysing the mind of the customer. The value of advertising. The value of window display. The value of training those in contact with the public. How best accomplished.

9. THE IMPORTANCE OF PUBLIC SPEAKING. —How to start. How to compile matter. How to construct a speech. The advantage of addressing the staff. The psychology you build up by addressing the whole staff together.

PRINCIPLES OF FINANCE

While Man Power is the most important factor in business, no business can develop far without money.

Most businesses fail because of their lack of ability to handle their finances successfully, just as a successful business wins through ability to make a profit.

Measure the success of your job or business by the net profit.

That word "net" is written deeply on the mind of every financier.

To secure net profit, your sales must be large enough to allow of a gross profit, that will pay all expenses, and leave a net profit for its owners.

There are profit leaks in a business. Learn to watch for them, and put new ideas in the Suggestion Box for the improvement of conditions.

Here are ten Profit Leaks in a business:

1. Customers lost through a lack of service, a lack of quality, or because the price is not right.
2. Raw materials bought badly (which is rare) or, what is more frequently the case, wasted in storage, and in operation.
3. A lack of prestige with the bank, and the general public. Money is easily obtained when the people have great confidence in you, as witness the ease with which Ford obtained his millions in England.
4. A lack of analysis of expenditure, and a watchful eye on increasing costs.

5. A lack of a costing system.
6. The absence of a business building department.
7. A lack of the team spirit and co-operation between all members of the staff.
8. A lack of keying results of advertising and other items of business building expenditure.
9. Insufficient or obsolescent machinery or equipment.
10. Too much hand or foot work, and not enough brain work.

PRINCIPLES OF ADMINISTRATION

Even if you are not in a position of authority, you can begin to learn the art of management.

Start on your own work, and your own department.

Here are some rules:

1. Have an understudy for every job.
2. Never do what someone else can do, even if they are slower.
3. Keep workers happy. Money is rarely the cause of a bad team spirit.
4. Be friendly, but not familiar with all those who work with you.

5. Think of the firm first, and so will the firm think of you.
6. Believe "there is a better way." Seek it.
7. Encourage everyone to take responsibilities, and to own up.
8. Whatever the price of what you sell, aim to improve the Quality.
9. Encourage yourself and others to use the Suggestion Box.
10. Keep fit. Many a sick manager makes a staff sick too, mentally and spiritually.

PRINCIPLES OF DISTRIBUTION

People must buy what your firm sells. Here are some tips that will help you widen the sphere of distribution:

1. List ten selling points of what the firm sells.
2. Suggest a new way to get more custom.
3. Can your sales service be improved? If so, how?
4. Can you use window displays profitably?
5. Do you issue attractive pieces of printed matter?
6. Have you a good series of sales letters?

7. Are your advertisements business builders?

8. Is your receptionist, your telephone clerk, carmen, credit clerk, office staff and factory folk conscious that they are all part of the selling plan?

9. Do you allow the public to visit your works? If not, why not?

10. Is 100% of enthusiasm maintained in your organisation?

PRINCIPLES OF SUPPLY

Everybody buys something. Most people buy when they need things, the wiser folk buy when the seller needs to sell.

If I buy an overcoat in October, I will pay 25% to even 40% more for it than if I buy it in March or April.

There is the buyer's market, when the supply is greater than the demand, and the price tends to drop; and the seller's market, when the demand is greater than the supply, and prices advance.

Part of your success will be the ability to buy in the best market.

Here are some tips on buying:

1. In a business only one man or his assistant should have authority to sign orders for purchases.

2. All stores should be kept like money, behind bars. You can save nearly 10% of raw material directly you have a stores system.
3. List all the goods you buy, and find out the best buying periods.
4. Don't buy too far ahead—never gamble in raw materials.
5. The credit buyer pays for it.
6. Second-hand material of times makes a second-hand job.
7. You can often effect savings by offering the staff half of all they save during the month. You get your full profit the second month.
8. Belong to your trade organisation. The other fellow has found out a saving you don't know about yet.
9. The cheapest is not always the best. You get what you pay for.
10. Keep accurate accounts. Take your discounts.

A GOOD SUGGESTION

Underline any of the forty points in which you are interested, and you will look at your job and business with new eyes and a happier interest.

CHAPTER THREE

PERSONAL PSYCHOLOGY ACTION AND RE-ACTION

LET us now embark for a while on to the sea of Human Nature.

It is a sea, for like the ocean, there are some depths still unplumbed, but much more is known today than in the past, and Science is still steadily pursuing its way, solving the mysteries, and enabling the layman to use the product of much research.

So psychologists all over the world are studying this problem of human nature, studying its actions and reactions.

Because you are studying Scientific Management, such an action is bound to have its reaction. Both on yourself and on others. Every action results in reaction. Your action has a reaction on to the mind of another, and in turn is the stimuli for the action on the part of another.

It is important then that we develop the right action, so that the reaction will be in our favour.

The more modern psychologists, please

remember, regard thought and emotion as part of the stimuli of action, so that action is here understood as "The expression of the personality in thought, word, and deed."

Reaction, a well-known dictionary informs us, means "to act again, to return an impulse, to act reciprocally, to resist by an opposite force, to act in opposition."

So that you see reaction has two effects: it can be either positive or negative.

It is, therefore, desirable in our study of human nature, that we take the positive attitude of mind, remembering that we shall not always achieve positive results, since the mind of the listener, or the mind of our objective, may not be in a positive state to receive our positive action, but the positive action is the only way to obtain positive reaction, since negative action nearly always reaps what it sows—negative reaction.

Our objective, then, is clear. It is to get positive action on the part of others, whether appealed to individually or collectively. So we at once embark on the amazing voyage of discovery of the reasons of human behaviour.

Let me, therefore, tell you how it is generally agreed the mind has developed.

It is assumed that the mind has developed to its present standard, and is developing to its higher standard through evolution, and that we have reached our present state of perfectedness through the instincts.

It would be as well, therefore, to study what are the primary instincts that have been responsible for the growth of human behaviour.

The instincts affect all of us, though it is true that the more immature the mind, the more the instincts predominate.

By studying the instincts, we shall be able to trace the growth of the mind, and so work up from the fountain springs of the mind to its present-day growth.

Primarily there are two great instincts:

1. Self Preservation.

2. Self-Perpetuation of the species.

Both instincts have had a great effect on the evolution of the race.

Broadly speaking, the instinct of self-perpetuation has to do with personal morality of the sexes, the attractive force of sex to sex, and the parental instinct, though the latter is governed by the other great cardinal instinct, self-preservation.

It is, therefore, by the analysis of the instinct of self-preservation, that we can gather so much that will be of use to us in projecting our personality towards others and inducing their actions to coincide with our wishes.

The instincts that spring from self-preservation are those instincts we inherit, and which are as old as the human race, and although we may, and do, differ from an intellectual standard, or an emotional standard, or from a volitional standard, we all, to a greater or less degree, possess the same innate tendencies or instincts.

It is to these innate tendencies we always appeal, when we appeal to the mass or crowd, and orators and agitators alike use these instincts when in contact with the crowd. The modern advertiser also is a master of crowd psychology, or to put it another way, has a keen understanding of the fundamental instincts that dominate the entire human race.

The development of the personality through education tends to inhibit or restrain action, or to develop the instinct by the introduction of higher mental forces, so that the instinct is the more easily gratified.

Every business man or woman ought to know the effect of the instincts on each individual.

It must be remembered that some instincts are stronger in some than in others, but we all possess them to some degree. The aim, therefore, in judging others, is to understand the exact instinct, or number of instincts, that dominate the personality you wish to analyse.

This is Mc Dougall's Definition of an Instinct:

"An instinct is an inherited or innate mental and bodily disposition which determines its possessor to perceive, and to pay attention to, objects of a certain class; to experience an emotional excitement of a particular quality upon perceiving such an object; and to act in regard to it in a particular manner, or at least, to experience an impulse to such an action."

Let us now analyse a few of the instincts, and note how the present-day personality of the average man grew out of these instincts.

THE INSTINCT OF CURIOSITY

In a child this instinct, as you know, is highly developed, and if it is not crushed or inhibited by unwise parents, this instinct, if developed, leads to analysis, or the asking of more and more questions, and so more and more knowledge, and more and more learning, then more and more experience, and finally, more and more wisdom.

You will notice a crowd is always curious, and so if you can arouse their curiosity sufficiently in your window displays, you have to get a policeman to move the crowd on. Instinctively we are all curious, and so if in our businesses we can make people curious, we have them thinking our way. So curiosity leads to interest, and if you want to make people interested, make them curious first. See how psychology begins to help you in the ordinary problems of life.

THE INSTINCT OF FEAR

Possibly this is the oldest and strongest of all instincts, and it is something that we all possess. We are all afraid of something. Though people may be curious, they sometimes inhibit their curiosity, because they are afraid of that which is new. In business, therefore, as in life, remember that people start afraid. It is as well, then, to build confidence with all your power, both in yourself and in your business, since confidence is the antidote of fear.

Actually we are always on trial. More people have expected us to take the petty cash than we shall ever realise.

The body is wonderfully formed to obey the instinct of fear. In the dawn of the human race, the fear instinct released forces that either stimulated us to run with rapidity out-side normal achievement, or froze us to an immobility so that not a muscle stirred. It is this instinct of fear that makes a hare run or stay petrified as though it were a stone.

The crowd mind possesses all sorts of fears, which are not existent in fact. The majority of people believe that jewellers steal jewels out of watches sent for repair, and that laundries have a special staff employed to tear the clothes, that all politicians are liars, and that all business men are rogues. This is but evidence of the outcrop of fear instinct finding an outlet of expression.

So that you can see how important it is in life, as in business, to create confidence, and to always provide an antidote to the fear instinct.

THE INSTINCT OF ACQUISITION

I know a wealthy old man who keeps the rind of oranges. "Some day," he says, "it will come in handy." There are people, like squirrels, who store much more than they can ever use. Yet this instinct of acquisition is with all of us and must be analysed.

We all have the instinct of wanting some-thing for nothing, though we have been so often deluded that people today are suspicious, because of the fear instinct, of the offer of something for nothing. But we all like a better price than our neighbours. We all like to be the specially favoured ones. We all like to possess, we all like to acquire. Hence the popularity of bargain sales, of lower prices. It is this instinct that makes us save, that makes us store. It is a powerful instinct to appeal to in business, if you can establish the confidence in your appeal.

THE INSTINCT OF CONSTRUCTION

Every child likes to make things. It will construct a tunnel out of a cardboard box and a bus out of a block of wood, in its own mind. We all of us have had experience of the desire to alter the conditions of life to our way of thinking, and so the instinct of construction builds the important mental habit of imagination.

So that when we appeal to people's imagination, we often go further and touch one of the main-springs of being. We go back to the instinct of construction.

It is this instinct that makes a child break open a drum to "see where the sound comes from," and to take a clock to pieces, if he is allowed, and often when he is not; and to hit a tap to pieces with a hammer to see how it stops the water.

The crowd always have this instinct of construction, and unless you educate them they build up their own plan of construction; hence, as already said, people believe that laundries have a special machine for tearing clothes, and that jewellers always take jewels from watches, that mechanics always leave motor-cars worse than they find them, and that doctors bury their mistakes.

So you will see the advantage of educating the public to your point of view, otherwise they will construct their own, which is as natural for them to do as it is to breathe.

PLEASURE AND PAIN

It is as well to remember and to understand what the magnetic poles of human contact are.

The two poles we alternately swing between are Pleasure and Pain.

We are always striving to swing away from the one and to the other. Yes, it is true that people will endure physical hardship (pain), but only to be rewarded subsequently in money or honours, or to be rewarded by an inward sense of satisfaction, which may be the aim of that individual, as, for instance, Amundsen in his polar flights.

Every human being, according to the development of his mentality, is seeking pleasure and avoiding pain.

Through the process of education we evolve our own standards of what consists of pleasure and pain. We often do things and put up with things, for an objective, such as a man going hungry in order to buy books, or a man working long hours in order that he may attain a bigger post, or acquire money for a motor-car.

In business therefore, of whatever nature, it is important that we recognise what is painful and what is pleasureable from the customer's point of view. We accentuate the pleasure and alleviate the pain if we are wise.

You will surely appreciate an increasing pleasure in the value of psychology. It is logical to conceive, too, that a painful act is likely to cause a painful reaction, and *vice versa*, with pleasure.

Not only in business, but with ourselves, we ought to analyse carefully that which gives us pleasure and that which gives us pain.

Here is a practical test.

Write down here:

I obtain most pleasure through

I am mostly pained through

Now write down what instinct gives you pleasure and what instinct causes the pain.

Favourable instinct

Unfavourable instinct

That is analysis, and by its means you can always analyse any situation in business or life, and build up your own philosophy, which is the surest way of achieving happiness in this life.

There are innumerable other instincts that

you can analyse, and which will build your mental contents, so that your mind will expand under the pleasureable experience of a ripe understanding.

HABIT

Fold a card once, and it will for ever hold the crease. Fold it twice, and the mark is more distinct; fold it a dozen times, and the card takes on a new shape. It is in two.

So habits change, alter, and destroy.

All life in the main is a matter of habits, and if we are successful in building up a right set of habits for ourselves and our businesses, success is sure.

It is our instincts which, moulded to thoughts, feelings and actions, build our habits, which make or mar us.

All efficiency instruction is based on the knowledge that reaction follows action, and that if the action suggested is sound, then the reaction will be right also.

It is reaction or habit that builds up repeat business. You have noticed how difficult it is to start a new idea, and how difficult it is to drop the old. It is this knowledge that makes the modern business man appreciate the law of habit, in order that business shall become as automatic as possible.

If one could devote time to a strict analysis of

our daily life, you would be amazed at the work of the law of habit. It is computed that for over 99.99% of the day we are under the control of habit.

This astonishing fact enables us to realise how beneficial it is to us to understand the habits of others, and our own, and so weave new and better habits into the fabric of the old.

So with others: get them to employ new habits. Of course, you will have difficulties, but be amused at this thought, that the time will come when they will fight as strenuously to retain, what you are now endeavouring to impart, with the same fierce intensity with which they attack that which is now new.

This is true of customers, as it is of Courts. It is as true of bankers as it is of butchers.

Do a thing once, and a new track is set up in the brain. Do it twice, and the track is deepened; do it a dozen times, and you have a habit; do it a thousand times, and you probably have a habit for life, and it may be so deeply impressed on you that you may pass its effect on to your descendants.

Always remember this, however: such is your power that no matter how deeply-rooted the habit may be, you have the power to change, alter, or destroy.

These brain tracks, or habits, are set up in the most pliable soil. This soil is nurtured by our instincts, our thoughts, feelings and strivings. So you see in everyone it is natural to form habits peculiar to their personality. This explains the natural tendency of some to control, and others to submit.

Fortunately, it is always to be remembered that we have the power of initiation. That is, we are masters of the situation. No matter what we are or where we are, if we will but start building new habits, for the old, automatically we can proceed to build success habits and success is ours.

There's the solution of personal psychology. Find out what causes your habits.

Then find out what causes the habits of your customers.

You are, then, well on the road to mastery.

CHAPTER FOUR

HOW THE MIND WORKS

AS Arnold Bennett says, the brain is the most magnificent instrument in the world.

The mental machine is capable, as I have already said, of tremendous development. The average man probably can expect, at least, a doubled efficiency as a result of studying this book, and improve the qualities of observation, comparison, concentration and judgment, which will help him to succeed in a more satisfactory way.

There are five gateways to the mind. These are the senses of sight, hearing, touch, taste and smelling. Of these, the keenest in 80% of cases is the sense of sight. Most of us gather raw material for the mind through the eye, and that is why in our advertising, in our conversations, in our selling and in our management, we should appeal to the eye as much as possible.

"Every picture tells a story" is a saying that is wonderfully true. Remember the human mind has grown from pictures. Intelligence was conveyed by pictures, and you can make a man understand and have him accept so much more by pictures than by a lengthy description in words.

As you will see in the sixth chapter, the mind retains these pictures in the sub-conscious mind, and a study of the sub-conscious mind is always worth while.

The human mind is 2% to 5% conscious and 95% to 98% sub-conscious.

The conscious is the now, and the sub-conscious is the past, and what is past always influences the future.

We are also under the influence of what we inherit. But the question of heredity is not so important as the question of environment. Environment shapes and moulds the human mind unconsciously to a tremendous degree. That is why Ford suggests, whenever he takes over any organization, that the first thing he believes in doing is, "clean up." He knows the value of environment.

You can only get clean work in a clean environment, and you can only get happy results in a happy environment, so you see your task is not only to help your mind grow, but to arrange conditions, as far as you can, so that other minds grow too.

THE MARVELLOUS MECHANISM OF THE BRAIN

The brain is the instrument of the mind, and

is the machine we use to express our thoughts, our emotions, and our will.

That is the problem, for as we think so we become, and if we improve our thoughts our results and actions will show the benefit of our thinking.

You will then understand that the raw material of ideas comes from what we see, what we hear, what we touch, what we smell, and what we taste.

There is no influence that comes to us through these five senses that doesn't affect the mind, first consciously, and afterwards sub-consciously.

Take this fact, for instance: When you first work in a noise, you notice it; in a week you become accustomed to it, for you no longer notice it at all.

Yet the sub-conscious mind, we know today through industrial fatigue research, notices the noise, and many nervous derangements have been caused through this recurring noise unnoticed by the conscious but yet received by the sub-conscious.

That is why I want you to understand the power of the sub-conscious mind, because it is so largely the force behind your habits.

Naturally, as a result of meeting together in this book, I want you to succeed, and so I want you to understand the remarkable forces you possess, and to help you shape your destiny.

If I can help you make your sub-conscious mind think success, it will act success, it will influence the whole personality to become success.

It is generally known today that the body is a marvellous network of telegraphic wires, and that every sensation received through the five senses travels to some centre of the brain for analysis.

If the sensation is one caused by a fly tickling your face, the automatic part of your brain will telegraph a reflect action to your hand, and you will probably attempt to "swat that fly." On the other hand, the sense of sight, as you now read, telegraphs to the brain, and because it is important the general manager of the brain will compare, and may cause the highest official (the Managing Director) to think and compare.

If it is important enough, the sensation thus passes to the Managing Director, who, like the General Manager, will call in from the files of the memory all information or stored sensations likely to help him in his comparison of this new sensation, and from this comparison there of times springs a new idea or judgment, and the Managing Director will then decide, and instruct the part of the body, generally the tongue or the hand, to carry out instructions, as a result of the first sensation caught through the eye, or it may be decided to store the sensation in the memory.

So that you see, observation, comparison, analysis, concentration and judgment, are all part of the work of the brain.

You cannot expect sound judgment from your mental machine, unless you have the requisite raw material.

You can either carry out someone else's instructions or your own. Most people prefer to do the former. For the hardest task in the world is to think.

Yet creative thinking, or initiative as it is sometimes called, is the one quality that brings a man out of the ruck.

Nearly all of us have to learn to obey. I always counsel beginners to learn quickly the art of obedience. Do as you are told, until you can find a better way, and then be sure to suggest the new way *tactfully*.

I know that workers can think of new ideas.

There are some minds that can think of new and valuable ideas for the business as easily as some learn to dance the latest dance.

You want new ideas, and I will tell you how you can train your brain to be your best servant.

READ MORE

Read a book about your job at least once a month. Take extracts—mark important passages, if the book is your own; if not, mark in pencil and then rub out.

WRITE MORE

After marking and extracting the meat from the book, write out your own thoughts about it.

Then compare what you have written with the extracts and marked passages.

As Bacon says, "writing maketh an exact man," and by writing your thinking becomes concrete.

That is why we ask you to answer the Test Questions, because by doing so you will have a concrete conception of the principles of these Text Books.

TALK MORE

Learn to talk about what you have written and read.

Join your Association or, if that is not possible, join a debating society and learn to speak on your feet.

This brings into the Arena of your own experience the experience of others.

This improves your reasoning.

When you learn a truth, you build that truth from proved facts—you thus reason deductively the scientific method and the method that modern business is using more and more.

A number of people reason inductively, and

then try to prove it.

They make a statement and endeavour to prove its truth—they reason backwards.

Deductive reasoning is longer but surer, and is reasoning upwards. This is the surer way to become a thinker.

Then, with a lot of practise, you learn to make swift judgment.

As the saying goes, your mind jumps to a decision. Your powers suggest to you a judgment which, when you set out to prove, you are right.

You may say "that business is bound to fail."

You may have so reasoned—deductively or inductively.

If you have been inside the business, studying it for months, your judgment is based on deductive reasoning.

If you are outside, you will have reasoned inductively from some observable phenomena.

The public largely reason inductively, hence the need for proof.

To say "our service is the best" does not convince the public, until you add "because," and then offer three or four proven facts.

So in offering suggestions, ideas, or exercising your initiative, be sure to reason deductively. Prove your case up to the hilt.

CONCENTRATE MORE

You will be well advised to read, write and talk about one subject at a time.

For instance, during this period you are actually studying human nature, so you will be advised to read books about Human Nature, Handling Men and Women, and Personal Psychology.

If you will write to me and tell me your position and work, I will gladly recommend what books to read.

Write about the subject, and select at least one friend to talk the matter over.

If an employer, select your most ambitious employee to study this book with you.

My experience is that a student can expect a doubled benefit by studying with an interested friend.

If you are an employee, find an ambitious friend, who is as keen as you are, and get him to read with you.

Thinking requires stimulation and encouragement, and so you want to manufacture the environment that will secure the highest percentage of result.

Remember always, "As a man thinketh so is he."

CHAPTER FIVE

THE MAGNETIC FORCE OF ENTHUSIASM

I AM a great believer in enthusiasm. I am sure, from my staff training experience, that this quality of personality is one that builds the team spirit more quickly than any-thing else I know.

So that you may capture my enthusiasm for enthusiasm, allow me to give you ten facts that prove conclusively of its value as a business-building asset.

(1) AN ENTHUSIASTIC MAN IS ALWAYS WELL

You will have noticed, as I have, that the enthusiast is brimful of energy and the joy of living, and that the enthusiast is never ill.

Enthusiasm is contagious. More sales, more work, less fatigue in the work, quicker results are obtained, and there is less annoyance, less grousing, and less risk of accidents when enthusiasm enters your business, and, of course, there is less illness.

When people have time to be sorry for themselves, then their efficiency drops alarmingly.

When a boy kicks a football aimlessly round a field, he soon gets tired.

But put him in a team, and he will play, strenuously for over an hour and hardly ever feel tired.

If his team is suffering a heavy defeat, the fatigue curve rises rapidly.

If his team is winning splendidly, he won't feel tired at all.

It is always the beaten crew in the Boat Race, that takes the longest to recover.

This significant fact leads us to the second suggestion.

(2) BE ON THE WINNING SIDE

Hide your failures from the staff and talk success. Hide your success from yourself, but face your failures, if you are strong enough to do so.

Every business executive knows that when the business is growing and expanding, more work at less cost, done in a happier spirit, often the result.

Contrary to popular opinion, a staff, like you and me, rejoice in that overload that makes us say "I don't know which way to turn."

Paradoxical as it may seem, a business is better off, when it is definitely on the down grade, than the stale business, because strenuous efforts are immediately made to put things right.

The difficult business is the jogging business. The one that is stale and has grown accustomed to itself.

Woolworth's, one of the most efficiently organised businesses in the world, change their managers every year. Rarely does a man stay two years in the same shop.

That efficiently organised religious body, the Wesleyans, also, through their circuit method, change the ministers to a new environment every few years.

The Commissioners of the Salvation Army are changed also at regular intervals.

To find the reason for this one has not far to seek, for you realise how stale you become without change, and new faces and new conditions soon effect a marvellous change in your point of view.

So keep your business busy. Don't allow it to grow stale, or give it time to notice itself.

Keep yourself busy, too. Better to have 1% overload than 10% underload.

Always keep work in hand. Keep the winning spirit abroad. Every month the staff should have a definite objective to fight for, so ought you.

This month sales, next month tidiness, next month economies, another month new customers, again a special advertising plan, and always a keyed-up sense of striving.

Again, tell the staff all about your successes. Keep your failures to yourself.

(3) ENTHUSIASM AND CONCENTRATION

Enthusiasm is the greatest concentrative force known. When you are enthusiastic, you lose sense of temperature, time and surroundings.

Nearly everyone, as a boy, has this spirit. As a model engineer, I lost all sense of discomfort and time—and I never recaptured this spirit until I became a salesman, and the thrill came back when I exerted myself sufficiently to win a gold watch in a world's selling competition.

I believe enthusiasm has to grow on you. Few love work at the beginning. It is only as we begin to become interested in our job that we grow to like it.

I am equally of the belief that few workers will be enthusiastic on their own. Their enthusiasm has to be manufactured. And the best way, from experience, is to give them an aim to accomplish.

Write down now a list of things you would like to see put right in your business, and watch your enthusiasm grow. If you are an employee ask your employer for six ways to improve your work, and go to him each month and ask for the verdict. Show your employer this book for your authority, otherwise he will wonder what has "bitten" you. Arouse enthusiasm, and you grow concentration.

(4) ENTHUSIASM AS A TONIC

When you are enthusiastic, you are younger, fitter, keener and more alert. And you are as happy as mortals can ever know happiness. Enthusiasm sees problems, instead of difficulties. Enthusiasm sees the possibilities, and not the impossibilities.

Enthusiasm makes you say "I can" and not "I can't." You can do more work, and do it more easily, when you are enthusiastic.

You can owe more money and expand your business when the spirit of the heart sings, which is but another term for enthusiasm. You dare more, and others dare with you. Success is a force that revitalizes itself. Your customers and workers catch the contagious spirit of enthusiasm alike, and exert themselves to build it bigger.

Enthusiasm makes us think of what will be, and not what won't be. Enthusiasm wins victories. Enthusiasm makes us tackle harder tasks and see joys in jobs that make pessimists quail.

Enthusiasm chloroforms "impossible."

(5) ENTHUSIASM BREEDS ACTION

Enthusiasm inspires activity. When you are enthusiastic you will start doing something. Enthusiasm finds relief in effort. Enthusiasm gives us the urge to accomplish. When you are enthusiastic you do not watch the clock, stop to grumble, or find time to criticise.

Enthusiasm sees the possibilities of life and gives you a concrete aim for every day, so that in the accomplishment of that aim you find new inspiration for the morrow. What else has made men leave their mark on history but their enthusiasm for a cause or creed?

For enthusiasm makes you forget self, and loses the "you" in the service for others. We know the other fellow's attitude of mind is the one we want to know, and enthusiasm enables us to find out what it is.

Enthusiasm alone is hot air, but allied to action it is superheated steam behind the cylinder—action. So you see the need of having a list of objectives.

I have noticed over and over again that directly we use graph charts for workers, and explain what they measure, the thin line begins to creep upwards, and even the most illiterate of workers begin to try to beat their previous best, all because they were given an objective to attain.

When a man says to his staff, "Let's do so-

and-so," and explains why, a new interest is at once abroad in the firm.

(6) ENTHUSIASM AS A MAGNET

When you are enthusiastic, you attract opportunities. The world gives its opportunities to those who do not need them. It is very difficult to get a job when you have not got one. When you are successful, everybody wants you.

The easiest business to organise, I find, is the one that has a waiting list of customers. The easiest man to find a better job for is the one who doesn't need the chance.

Success breeds success. That is why I have always found it policy to push a business for all it is worth when it is succeeding. It is ever so much easier. Everybody in the business is a better salesman, and that fatal obstacle to success—over-anxiety—is certainly absent.

When you want a thing badly you tend to betray your personal desire, sometimes selfish, for your objective.

When the personal element is lessened, you tend to think more of your customer or client. When anxiety is out of the mind, enthusiasm has a chance to rear its head triumphantly. For it is true, we attract what we are. If we are full of troubles, we only gather more. We betray ourselves in our weaknesses, only to have the load added to. If you are feeling "licked," others try to beat you with harsher blows. That is why it will pay you to drive pessimism and dullness out of your personality, and think, dream and act success. Even dress yourself the success you want to be.

So even if your spirit is a little bowed down, as you read this, you must lose it in the thought of success for now and ever. Dispel this gloom (for as long as you indulge in it but manufactures more) by reading optimism, then talking it to the first man who wants to be mournful, and then writing about it, at the first opportunity. In a month you are different. People notice it, too, and their opinion always agrees with your own. Say your business is in a rotten state, and people believe you.

Say you are a success, and people won't believe that either at first, but act success, and people flock to your standard. So your talk, your actions, your attitude, the appearance of you and your business, your letterheads, your printed matter, and your advertisements must all reflect your success.

Do they? Have a look.

(7) ENTHUSIASM IS THE SOLVENT OF DIFFICULTIES

Enthusiasm, you will find, transforms your difficulties into problems. Every job in the world has its troubles. I do meet people who hope that tomorrow, next week, or next year, will be the time when there will be less and less troubles and anxieties, when the law of life is that the older we grow the more troubles we get. No one has ever avoided them. The only way to handle them is to do as the Scotsmen do with thistles—grasp them tightly.

Enthusiasm makes you walk towards the real jobs of life.

(8) ENTHUSIASM BEGETS FAITH

Faith is the centre half behind the centre forward of enthusiasm. Enthusiasm scores goals, but Faith sustains enthusiasm in defeat. Part of the value of this book to you is that you will build a greater faith in your belief in ultimate success.

Whether you are an owner, or manager, or going to be, you will need tremendous enthusiasm. When you lead, or aspire to do so, there is so much one has to overcome, so the reserve force of faith is needed.

Enthusiasm with its energy keeps Faith alert, and that is another advantage to be gained by the cultivation of enthusiasm.

(9) ENTHUSIASM INCITES THE IMAGINATION

You will have gathered by now that Enthusiasm is a great inciter. One of its big effects is that it makes the VISION clearer and nearer. You will agree with me a year from now that you have attained more, won more victories, and that you are leagues nearer to your great objectives.

Enthusiasm is the oxygen of the soul. It has ever inspired men to dare with that faith that surmounts the facts of life. Why not you, too?

(10) ENTHUSIASM MAKES US UNDERSTAND

Because enthusiasm is an active force, and gives you the urge to accomplish, it actually drives you in contact with more and more people. Once the momentum of enthusiasm is started, it generates its own forces for higher accomplishment.

The urge of enthusiasm makes men understand. Because they want to accomplish so much they need to seek the co-operation of their fellows, and must understand the heads and hearts of mankind. Enthusiasm is a great teacher. It brings its own rebuffs, and its own lessons, and we are driven willy-nilly to understand. Minds are lethargic. Hearts are cold, and hands are lifeless.

Enthusiasm reinvigorates all three—you will find enthusiasm is useful to you in your success, as the Cup Winners find encouragement in their own supporters.

CHAPTER SIX

MEMORY TRAINING

MEMORY has been recognised from the days of the ancients as one of the greatest of mental attainments, and the modern business man recognises it as a great asset. Millions have said, "I forgot." We all must acknowledge our failure at times.

Everyone has a good memory for something. I recall an incident that proves this statement. I was asked by an executive, "I wish you could do something for John," indicating a smart-looking lad, who seemed bright enough. "John," said his chief, "has the worst memory of anyone I know."

So I wandered over and had a word with this bright-looking youngster. "Son," I asked him, "which is your favourite football team?" "Arsenal," he answered, somewhat shyly, wondering, I suppose, what was the idea. "And who is the Captain now?" He knew, and also the team members of last Saturday, the transfer fees they had cost, the position of the team in the league, and he knew a lot more about the club than the average man would ever know. In other words, he was interested, and interest is the secret of all memory retaining and recalling.

If you are interested, you can remember, and so that is one of the great benefits of staff training, for it arouses interest among the workers, and with this new interest there is immediately a new spirit in the organisation.

Memory is a storehouse, and, like all good storehouses, the contents should be classified and organised. There are wider and better-lighted entrances to the storehouse than others. We have five altogether—THE EYE—THE EAR —THE SENSE OF TOUCH—TASTE—and THE SENSE OF SMELL. The Eye is the widest and best-lit entrance to the memory.

Most people are eye-minded, nearly 80% as a matter of fact, so that if you want your advertisement or instruction to be remembered, note that "every picture tells a story."

I have carried out this experiment so often in staff training to be thoroughly convinced of the keenness of the eye.

Provide all members of the audience with pencil and paper, and then proceed to show them twenty articles from a suitcase, and then give them two minutes to write out the list of all they can remember. Anyone with a good visual memory can recall eighteen of the articles, and on that test is 80% efficient. Then test the same audience in the same way, but read to them twenty words, and it is rarely that you get 70% efficiency.

Ask those to hold their hands up who have remembered more articles than words, and 90% of those present will vote for eye-mindedness.

Most people will tell you they cannot remember poetry, so I write on the blackboard:

"It matters not how straight the gate,
How charged with punishment the scroll,
I am the Master of my Fate,
I am the Captain of my Soul."

I then ask the audience to write this verse down on paper. Then I ask them to tear the paper up. I say a few words about Henley, the writer of the poem, and turn to them suddenly and ask them to write out the verse that they had written down, and I find that dozens can repeat it on request.

Why? Because they have concentrated; so interest, allied to concentration, increases memory efficiency.

Here is another interesting fact about the memory. The mind automatically links concepts together. For instance, a series of words as on the left are hard to remember, but note how easy when linked as on the right:

Steam	Laundry
Height	Steam
Heat	Heat
Floor	Presses
Water	Ironers
Ironers	Height
Valves	Floor
Concrete	Concrete
Sales	Water
Roof	Valves
Work	Leaks
Building	Roof
Training	Glass
Prismatic	Prismatic
Laundry	Light
Glass	Work
Happiness	Increase
Leaks	Happiness
Light	Bonus
Bonus	Profit
Increase	Building
Presses	Sales
Profit	Training

To show how the mind links together concepts which remind one of the other, here is an explanation of the right-hand column:

Laundry Steam	Cause and effect, and effect and cause.
Steam Heat	Cause and effect, and contents.
Heat Presses	Contiguity (one is where the other is).
Presses Ironers	Contrast.
Ironers Height	Correspondence and contrast. (Some ironers are too short in height for bench, but all benches are same height.)
Height Floor	Cause and effect. (Board on floor, according to height of worker, makes for greatest efficiency.)
Floor Concrete	Correspondence and contents.
Concrete Water	Contiguity (invariably there is too much water on the floors of laundries in the wash-house owing to insufficient camber).
Water Valves	Cause and effect, contiguity, and contents.
Valves Leaks	Cause and effect. (Valves invariably leak in inefficient laundries.)
Leaks Roof	Effect from cause.

Pair	Relation
Roof Glass	Contents (modern laundries are using glass roofs).
Glass Prismatic	Contents (prismatic glass gives the best light for laundries).
Prismatic Light	Cause and effect, and contents.
Light Work	Cause and effect. (The better the light, the higher the standard of work.)
Work Increase	Cause and effect (in view of conditions above).
Increase Happiness	Cause and effect (workers are happier the busier they are).
Happiness Bonus	Cause and effect (for the owner becomes happier too, as a result of increased work, and thinks out some plan of bonus).
Bonus Profit	Cause and effect (bonuses mean more profit, for they pay, and increase the efficiency).
Profit Building	Cause and effect (the more profit, the greater the inducement to build and enlarge).
Building Sales	Cause and effect (the larger the building the more need for sales).
Sales Training	Cause and effect (the more need for sales, the greater the need for training).

I have given the explanation how these points were linked in my mind, and you will notice that I used five links:

1. Cause and effect.
2. Contrast.
3. Correspondence.
4. Contents, part or whole.
5. Contiguity.

You will find that the memory uses these five links to classify all that it wishes to remember. This is known as "The Association of Ideas," and, as you will have read, we learn to associate either by:

1. Cause and Effect, as, for instance, my sore thumb reminds me of the garden where I fell and dislocated it.

2. Contrast reminds me of the finest-lit laundry I have ever seen, compared with the darkest.

3. Correspondence I use, when I see a brown laundry van, for I am reminded of Mr. Brown, the proprietor.

4. Contents is the law I used when I remember that the London Press Exchange is in the same street as the Coliseum.

5. Contiguity is the law that operates when I always remember to hang my umbrella on the same peg as my hat.

These are but simple illustrations, but they serve to illustrate how the mind works in a wonderful way to classify its mental contents. The three aids, as you will notice, are:

Interest,
Concentration,
and
Association.

Alliteration is another aid to memory training, as, for instance, "Beecham was born in Bristol," or "Brown lives at 49, Barnes Park."

FOR PUBLIC SPEAKERS

The principle of initialisation is often used by Public Speakers, and it can be used in other ways as well.

Supposing that you wish to speak on "Management." Using the word as a key, you could compile your points as follows:

M man power, the biggest problem in business.
A awards necessary in money and praise.
N nuisances to managers.
A ability can be developed by managers.
G girl problem.
E efficiency is personal before collective.
M man handling
E enthusiasm to be developed by manager.
N natural aptitude to be found by manager.
T tact, the exquisite quality.

Some memories seem to have a natural quality of remembering in this way, and it is a method I have used very successfully, and, after practise, it is quite easy to speak for an hour without notes.

TEN TIPS ON MEMORY

1. Never attempt to remember when the body is tired. You will find that you have a peak point of memory. At one time of the day your brain is fresher and more retentive than any other.

2. When memorising, you will find that you will need rest periods. Some rest five minutes every quarter of an hour. Others find that five minutes every hour is sufficient.

3. Memory is impaired by too much tea, coffee, alcohol, exercise, and, above all, by worry and strain.

4. If you wish to remember a name, say it, write it down, and visualise it. Suppose you wish to remember the name "Bennett," and you had met a stout grocer of that name many years ago in Muizenberg, you could picture it in your mind by the joviality of your old friend, and either by correspondence; say to yourself, "Bennett, yes, you remind me of big Bennett, you smile just like him";

or you could say by contrast, "You are as miserable as big Bennett was happy."

5. When reading a worth-while book, as you finish a page, shut the book and endeavour to recall what has been written. If you cannot, read it again. This trains the mind to concentrate.

6. The following exercise has been pronounced to be one of the finest known for mind training. It is to go over, at the end of the day, all the important incidents that have happened. A sort of exercise we indulge in after a happy holiday, when we live each day over again in our minds. Happy memories, we call them, and if we only kept up this exercise, in three months we would notice a perceptible difference.

7. You cannot retain what you have not obtained. The memory cannot recall what you have not written on the tablets of the memory, hence the importance of concentration when you wish to remember.

8. Don't try and remember two things at once. Some do, and then miss both.

9. Trust yourself. Use Auto-Suggestion. Never say, "I am sure to forget this." You are but commanding your sub-conscious self to do so.

10. Learn to rely on the memory. Ever had this experience ? You meet a man, but you cannot recall his name, and the more you try to recall it, the farther off it seems, yet an interesting turn of the conversation made you forget the search for the name for the moment, and then suddenly the name pops into the mind.

It pays to rely on the memory, so if there is something you wish to recall, say to it, "Memory, find the name of that chap over there," and forget the command, and your Memory will work for you sub-consciously.

A final tip: Develop a "forgettery "as well as a memory.

Learn to forget snubs, slights, disasters, losses, and catastrophes.

Use this great gift of memory to retain and recall only the brightness and happiness of life. In other words, the best aid memory can be to you is to have you always look on the bright side of things.

CHAPTER SEVEN

EFFICIENCY PRINCIPLES

PLANS

A LAUNDRY I know recently purchased a plot of land adjacent to their present plant. At once the thought arose—what to do with the land?

Immediately came discussion, and then planning started. With pencil and paper, suggestions were first made in a broad sense, and then transferred to paper in a concrete sense.

So presently there was evolved a plan or scheme of what to do, before a spade was used or a brick laid.

Because the plan has been analysed by twelve astute minds, the future has been fore-cast, and mistakes avoided. So ought all business to be conducted: "Work your plan, plan your work."

WASTE

Waste is an unpardonable crime in a business-like organisation. There is waste in man-power, materials, methods, machinery, time and money.

Time is probably the greatest waste of them all.

The plan is used to save time.

The easiest way to test this is, to plan tonight what you will wear tomorrow. If you are changing a suit, take another off its hanger tonight. Choose a harmonious tie, the right collar, a clean handkerchief, and anything else you need, and see how easily you can dress on the morrow.

Take a lesson from the ladies. A well-dressed woman always plans what she will wear and how, and gets everything ready before she commences to dress.

As you plan your personal dress, so can you plan your own work, until you develop the habit so well that you can *plan* the work of others, which is the next step, after standards, to the realisation of scientific management.

PLANNING SALES

If it is desired to increase sales 10%, it is first necessary to set the standard, and then sub-standards, for each person responsible for sales. This is known as setting a quota.

It is a curious psychological effect that if you plan to sell all you can, it is not so effective as setting up a figure, even though the latter is set much higher than the expectancy of the former.

So it pays to establish standards, and then plan to obtain them.

A salesman with a new standard, or quota of 10% increase of sales, resolves to increase sales with each customer 10%, if that is feasible and good service, and may, in addition, determine to add so many new customers to his list. Not as many as he can get, but a definite number fixed in his mind, say one a day for a week, or twenty a month.

All the most successful sales managers constantly set quotas.

If you have anything to obtain out of life, set the standard, and then plan how and why to get it.

The salesman with a quota has a definite goal, which generally looks impossible of accomplishment.

Anything new is generally difficult of accomplishment, but the plan begins to introduce the shorter, easier and better way.

Soon the standard is attainable, and either loafing or yearning sets in. Some workers loaf on attaining the standard, others look for new fields to conquer. It is the latter who win the prizes of the world, but the former type of mind teaches us that standards in business are, with the exception of the moral, subject to constant change and improvement.

So no standard should be set up in the spirit that it is unalterable or unchangeable.

Scientific planning will always show higher and higher possibilities of attainment, and in no way is that so apparent as in planning for sales.

Sales are the greatest variable in business. They are usually the greatest expandable factor. Because selling is the hardest of all tasks in business, it is generally neglected, but the institution of planned standards soon sets things moving. Try it.

PERSONAL PLANNING

Have you ever started the day with a plan only to find some unplanned effect spoilt it all ?

Did you say, "Ugh, planning is of no use," and then discontinue ?

Or—

Did you persevere at planning?

If the latter, you will agree how important the plan has become.

First of all, you started planning a day in advance. In a month you probably found yourself planning a week in advance, in a year you found yourself planning a month ahead, and today you have so far advanced in the art that you can plan at least a year or more ahead.

One wants to practise planning. For that reason the Yearly Success Chart is included in this chapter.

Planning, as you will understand now, is looking ahead.

I want you to look ahead for a year.

I want you to write under the heading, "Health," all the things you determine you will do to keep fit, such as walk an hour a day, drink eight glasses of water, or at least one in the morning and one at night. Promise yourself to eat fruit and green vegetables, and to be regular in your habits.

Under the heading "Knowledge," I want you to write out what you will do in order to get that knowledge you deem essential for your well-being. Whether it is a knowledge of dancing or economics, you must plan to arrange lessons, maybe obtain books, and arrange hours for practise or study.

Under the heading "Power," you would write those plans which will result in people doing what you wish. Whether you want leadership in a football team or in a factory, you have heights to scale, difficulties to over-come, and obstacles to surmount. At least plan to overcome these dangers, and you, with your trained mind, will be bound to succeed.

"Prestige" is your influence you leave behind you.

Plan how you will increase its effect. Four factors developed will always increase prestige — to think—to be courageous—to keep fit— and to *do* things.

Plan how to develop these four divisions of personal prestige.

MONEY

Wise spending is the highest form of thrift. It is all a matter of planning.

At the end of this chapter you will find Efficiency Chart No. 12.

Keep this chart for a week, or get your wife to keep it. At the end of that time, cross out in blue pencil the expenditures you could have done without. This helps you start a reserve—by keeping back money spent in unnecessary ways.

You can never plan while you owe. The debtor is a slave to the creditor. If not in walls, the debtor is in a mental pen, and nothing builds confidence so quickly and positively as having a financial reserve. The art of making money resolves itself to one rule alone: "Money Makes Money," and it doesn't matter how little you have, it will make some more for you.

Money is the greatest magnet in the world. The more money you possess, the more you can get. £100 attracts another £100. £1,000 will attract £10,000. £10,000 will attract £100,000. £100,000 a million, and with a million you can attract all the money there is.

So plan to save, even though a shilling a week. It gives a power, force and magic that nothing else can replace.

As "Money Makes Money," keep some.

PLANNING FOR OTHERS

A manager, foreman or charge hand should, with the red fire of enthusiasm, make a beacon light of the word "action."

In other words, "Keep things moving."

It is folly to allow idle workers or idle machines. Both deteriorate much more rapidly when idle than when fully engaged at work.

Planning is the only effective means to prevent idle machine hours and wastage of labour. Workers rarely think for themselves, and it devolves on to the manager or foreman to do the thinking for the workers.

In some organisations where Scientific Management has been fully developed, planning has grown to the extent that machines are tabbed, and under each tab will be found in the planning office, work set out for each machine, with every job fully and completely demarcated, time to start—to stop—material required, tools, jigs, etc.

In the same way, under wise management, each worker can have work allocated ahead, either by records kept on cards or books.

So, to plan for others, you must possess something of the prophetic sense. The capacity to peer ahead for the "blind "ones of the earth. Look ahead!

PLANNING IN THE OFFICE

Once a year every member of the office staff should plan to do this. Empty out every drawer of every desk and discard the useless.

Every file should be gone over, and the "dead wood" transferred.

Every cupboard should be overhauled and tidied.

Every loose thing in the office should have a place, and its home labelled.

A nail and a label "telephone directory" works wonders.

Plan the contents of your drawer in the same way by writing out labels of the contents. Do the same for all homeless articles in an office, post box—string—rubber stamps —special books.—just have a look at your office now, and note the "lost sheep."

The office manager, once a year, should draw a ground plan of his office space, cut out of cardboard models of desks to scale, lay out the plan on his own desk, and satisfy himself that he is using all the office space in the most efficient way, testing this through trying his cardboard models in different positions.

For this reason, unnecessary walking, reaching or stretching, can be eliminated by planning.

Planning has enabled a ledger clerk to do 50 per cent, more work easier, because conditions were standardised and a plan evolved to do the most work with less fatigue.

Typists can do more work with a plan than without one.

Indeed, planning never ceases. Its fountain head should be in the office, so that all may behold the wonderment of planning.

Does your office show the rest of the organisation—how?

PLANNING IN THE FACTORY

Planning, in the scientific management understanding of the word, reaches its highest form in the factory.

I have said that there is a waste in man-power, materials, methods, machinery, time and money.

I have found all these wastes in one factory.

Here is a suggestion that will help you at once to check up wastes, if any, in your factory.

Follow a flow of work through the factory from its raw state to the finished product.

Keep track of this work by means of a chart. Procure the largest of white drawing paper sheets and pin it on a board. Note when the work starts and where—trace all its movements on the chart in exact scale to its actual movements.

While the work is moving, draw a straight line and note the time and length of movement. While the work is stationary, that is, while it is being worked upon say by a machine, draw a square on your chart to represent the halt.

When your chart is completed you will have a series of lines and squares.

You now start investigating. Concentrate on each square, until you are satisfied there is no waste in man-power, materials, methods, machinery, time or money.

William G. Fern, F.R.S.A.

EFFICIENCY ENGINEER

11, Upper Woburn Place, Southampton Row, London, W.C.I.

ANALYSIS OF EXPENDITURE
EFFICIENCY CHART No. 12

Week Commencing	SUN	MON	TUE	WED	THU	FRI	SAT	REMARKS
FOOD								
Groceries								
Vegetables								
Fruit								
Meat								
RAIMENT								
Clothes								
Boots								
Repairs								
Laundry								
SHELTER								
Rent								
Furnishing								
Lighting								
Heating								
Servants								
PERSONAL								
Studies								
Books and Papers								
Smoking								
Refreshments								
Amusements								
INVESTMENTS								
Clubs								
Societies								
Savings								
Insurance								
EMERGENCIES								
Doctor								
Chemist								
Charities								
SUNDRIES								
Trams (1)								
Trains (2)								
(3)								
(4)								
(5)								
Totals								Week's Total

Examine carefully each week's expenditure and cut out all items that do not give full value for money spent.

Yearly Success Chart....................19..........
The Five big Factors for Success are Health, Knowledge, Power, Prestige and Money Plan now what you will do this year to add to all five
To enjoy HEALTH I will—
To add to my KNOWLEDGE I will—
To add to my POWER I will—
To add to my PRESTIGE I will—
To add to my MONEY I will—
SPECIAL

CHAPTER EIGHT

STANDARDISED CONDITIONS AND OPERATIONS

WE are now embarking on to the greater adventure.

This will be the chapter which will tell you how to use the principles of Scientific Management in a detailed way, and to effect what may be apparently miraculous improvements of operations and conditions.

The Father of Scientific Management, as you know, was the late Dr. Winslow Taylor, and you should read at some future time the two interesting volumes on his life.

Taylor was the first man who said there was a Science behind Management, as there was a science behind any art, when the rules and laws had been carefully organised and tabulated.

Evolving out of his research, came the fundamentals that in every business were Standardised Conditions and Standardised Operations which, when sought for, would lead to an economy of production, resulting in three attainments.

First, that by means of the above two principles and others, costs would be lowered.

Second, rewards would be increased.

Third, that the interest of the worker would be sustained, and thereby harmonious contentment would reign, without which life is a negation.

All this has been proved to be true, and, furthermore, where Scientific Management has been introduced with loyal faith, costs have been lowered, profits increased, prices lowered, and wages increased, so that employer, employee and consumer have all benefited.

This has been the result of the application of the principles which we are now studying.

The Science of Management, as it is now understood, takes this stand. Because a condition has existed for a long period, and has become hallowed by age, it does not necessarily mean that that condition is right. Nor, because an operation has been performed in a certain way for a hundred years, is it necessarily right either.

STANDARDISED CONDITIONS

It is better understood today how necessary it is to establish the right conditions in order to obtain the maximum of efficiency. There are four great considerations. They are: Light, Heat, Ventilation, and Work Zone.

It is absolutely proved that the best results are obtained from workers who have the right light. As far as is possible, light should come over the left shoulder on to the work, without shadows, and should be diffused. Workers should not be faced with the full glare of either daylight or artificial light. I have seen a worker facing an electric light, all day long, with it about twelve inches from his nose. On asking the worker if he suffered from head-aches, I was not at all surprised to learn that he did. Yet he had never connected his head-aches with the bad lighting effect. That was not the worst, however. This worker had an unenviable record for errors, yet when lighting conditions were altered for him his record of reliability rapidly increased. See, then, that any workers under your control have the benefit of as good lighting conditions as possible. All inspection work, for instance, must be performed in the right light and under the right conditions.

Light, like heat and air, has a great effect on the human body. We speedily feel the extremes of heat and cold. Yet there is some-thing more subtle. It must always be remembered that the human system is wonderfully accommodating, and that it will gradually accustom itself to anything, even to living in a dungeon for a number of years. So a slight difference in the temperature, while noticeable at the commencement of the day, goes un-noticed, like bad air, for the rest of the period. It has been proved by test that even a slight difference of temperature has an effect on the workers. Ten degrees one way or the other has a deleterious effect. The correct temperature for any working place is 63 degrees. It is not always possible to establish this temperature, but means can be taken in the construction of a new building to aim at this standard.

The time will come when all work places will be automatically heated or cooled, according to the outside prevailing temperature. As is well known, the more up-to-date woollen mills maintain an even temperature in their works all the year round.

So much is known today about the value of fresh air that little need be said on this important point. Suffice it to say, that unless the right air is present, workers will speedily become fatigued, and that is but a short cut to errors, irritation, and slight physical ailments, causing in the long run a greater cost than the first cost of organising the right supply of air.

I have been on the top of a large building where the flat roof has been made into a playing ground for the workers, who are required, when the weather permits, to spend their rest periods there. You may regard this as rather arbitrary, but workers are not always keenly alive to what is best for them, and at times it must be remembered that they have to be led to do those things which are good for them, which, when left to themselves, would never be done.

Establishing the Right Work Zone is, of course, very important. Ford, when he bought his railway, was asked what was the first thing he was going to do. He replied, "Clean up." And clean up he did. Rubbish was burnt, dark places whitewashed, until one worker said, "there's no place to spit here." Ford has always regarded that remark as one of the greatest compliments he has ever received.

So, in many an organisation, would the advice of "clean up" be sound. Not only should time be spent on Saturday morning for this work, or Monday morning if you wish, but at least one week a year should be spent in a general spring clean. Working in the same place day after day, under the same conditions, one does not notice how things can become more and more grimy, and more and more untidy. Workers will always take on their environment. Give them clean surroundings, and they will be clean. Give them hovels, and they grovel. So in business, cleanliness is not only before godliness, but before profits as well.

Each worker has a work zone, and the main principle to have in mind is that this zone should be restricted as is compatible with efficiency. Under the principles of Standardised Operations, much will be said as to the details of application. The instinct of owner-ship is strong in all of us, and this should be appealed to in handling workers. Make them individually responsible, therefore, for as much as you can. Get them to talk about "my machine," "my locker," but "our" factory, "our" customers, and "our" business.

STANDARDISED OPERATIONS

It is well-known today that bodily fatigue speedily reacts on the mind, and the new thought in organisation today is to save the body unnecessary movements and to avoid awkward angles of working, and to lessen mistakes and inefficiency.

This is the great difficulty of altering present standards of operations. Workers have grown so accustomed to do what they have to do, in the way they do it, that any other way is looked upon as the wrong way, whereas the chances are 100 to 1 that their way is the wrong way, since their actions are self taught, and their operations at best but copied from others, who in turn copied their methods from older men still. Since it is rare that these movements have been the means of intelligent study, you are safe to assume that any method of operation, unless scientifically studied, is WRONG.

In studying operations, the first thing to watch is that no operation is performed by anyone, if someone less skilled and less highly paid can do it as well. Walking should be eliminated as much as possible, but if it has to be done let some lower paid worker do it.

Time and time again I have watched highly

paid workers wander round looking for something, or seeking an instruction, when someone whose time was less valuable could have done the necessary work equally as well. Instructions, in any case, should always be put in Writing. The unnecessary irritation and internal litigation that is experienced in organisations could be eliminated by this one principle alone.

It is better that work should be brought to the worker, than the worker to the work.

It is better to feed the worker with the necessary tools and equipment than for the worker to fend for himself. This applies to typists as well as to skilled machine workers. Many a highly skilled typist searches for stationery and paper, when a junior could do the work equally as well. Thought alone can determine how these effects can be attained, but suffice to say that essentials only should be handled by the essential workers, and the non-essential by the non-essential.

Unnecessary movements should be eliminated both in the flow of the work through the organisation as well as in the operations at each station of work.

To properly study the working conditions of any organisation, it is first necessary to prepare a ground plan to scale of the place of working, whether an office or a factory. On this plan should be drawn every desk used, as well as every piece of furniture or machine or other equipment.

If an office, it would be as well to trace the travel of a letter, for instance. This line of travel could be faintly traced on the ground plan in pencil. If this has never been done before, it is surprising to note the criss-crossing that takes place, and immediately by an intelligent rearrangement of equipment much time would be saved.

To illustrate how time can be unintelligently wasted, and unknowingly, too: I remember once in an organisation the following incident. It was an office of quite a large floor space, seating about 300 clerks. At one end of the room was a drinking fountain, one of the new kind in which the water spurted upwards so as to avoid contamination.

As this was an organisation which believed in hygiene, workers had been taught many valuable points, amongst them, to drink plenty of water. They did, hour after hour. But on calculation it was ascertained that the staff, to get that water, walked nearly 400 miles per annum. By the rearrangement of the fountains much of this unnecessary waste was eliminated.

Too many offices look too pretty. Everything seems to be well arranged on well co-ordinated lines. Furniture is set out as though it were in a drawing room. Everything seems to have to match. Others again look as though the furniture is where the movers left it. Neither is right. The equipment of any organisation, factory or office should be placed in that position where the most efficient working results can be obtained.

The ground plan will, then, lead to a re-arrangement of desks and equipment in order to save lost motion.

Note the flow of work through. It should travel as straight as possible. This may involve a rearrangement of machines, but even this is cheaper than to pay labour for unnecessary movements. Labour costs are always the highest cost in any business. So the line of travel should be as straight as possible without any retracing.

The next point to observe is to note whether that line of travel can be made shorter or quicker. Gravity chutes and conveyor belts are used in order that work may travel from point to point more quickly than it would otherwise do. The newer organisations are always studying such points, since material in process costs money in capital when travelling and nothing is happening to it. In how many organisations do you know that the only solution they have for a rush is to engage more labour, when a rearrangement would speedily effect the required speed-up?

We now reach the point where most economies can be effected, not only in your business, but in almost every business in the land.

This is to watch the operations at each station. (A station is a place where the work stays to have some operation performed upon it.) This can be done with everyone's work. The only possible exception may be that of an executive who has to think, but even he has to study conditions in order that his brains will operate at their highest function.

Psychologists state that the mind is at its highest activity when the body is climbing an easy uphill woodland path, but all executives cannot adjourn to woods to think, so they must establish their own methods of standardised conditions in order that they may operate at the highest efficiency. Some may think better with the door locked. Others in contact with the staff, others when walking through the business, others when playing billiards. Other men have told me that they think best in their baths.

Nearly every man has his own particular environment and set of conditions when he can think better than at any other time. Seek such conditions for yourself, it will pay you.

On the other hand, it is to be remembered that you have certain routine things to do. In other words, there are certain things you have to perform day after day that should be standardised for conditions and operations until you arrive at the best, easiest and quickest way of doing them.

Probably one of the best ways to teach yourself the necessity of the study of operations is to watch others at work. Look at a typist at work. Note if she is seated comfortably, at the right height, with the proper foot rest. You may say this is pampering the worker, but we know that bodily fatigue creates mental fatigue, and that the physical ache is communicated to you when you get the letters to sign. Note if the lady has to search, fetch or carry. Note even the operations of the typewriter. If the lady is a touch typist, that is, one who operates the keys without looking at the key-board, she is fifteen per cent, more efficient than her sister who does not.

Go into the factory. I have seen tall people stooping down to a job, and short people reaching upwards. The proper bench height even is important in order to avoid bodily fatigue.

Some workers reach too far. Any awkward movement even should be avoided in order that the workers should not experience that tired feeling.

Do you know one of the best ways to get better methods of operations? It is to adopt the suggestion box idea. Locked up in the mind of every worker are ideas which will make for better operations. Offer prizes for the best suggestions, and send a letter of thanks to all those who send in an idea.

So you see these methods enable you to arrive at even higher standards than those established in our first chapter. Having done this, reduce the story of each job to writing. Be sure to reap the benefit of such study. Put it down in writing for the benefit of the next worker, and so the newcomer is speedily transformed into an efficient worker in a remarkably short space of time.

You now realise how progressive Scientific Management is. You first set Standards in order to have something to aim at.

We then study the principle of Planning in order that we might arrive at even higher standards of attainment, endeavouring to eliminate waste in material and effort.

Now we have carried you a step further by introducing you to the details of the principles of Standardised Operations and Standardised Conditions, and I am sure you have much work in front of you of a fascinating nature.

In a previous chapter we discussed with you the important psychological principle of ACTION AND REACTION. By now you are firmly convinced as to the growth of psychology in business. It is the newest of all sciences, and it is being applied more and more every day in the more up-to-date businesses.

I can promise you that the next chapter will be as interesting as any you have ever read, and immensely profitable.

CHAPTER NINE

SALES PSYCHOLOGY

THERE is a silent revolution apparent in Great Britain.

Every thinking person is beginning to believe that there is something in salesmanship, that salesmanship does not just happen. Moreover, the rising executive knows that salesmanship can be taught just as mathematics can be taught, and that while some have a natural tendency for "maths.," others have a natural tendency for selling.

But this profound truth has also become apparent: that just as everyone needs so much figuring to get along in the world, so is it true that everyone who wants to be anyone needs so much salesmanship, if they would succeed to the full extent of their possibilities.

Sales psychology, therefore, deals with salesmanship in the broadest possible way.

It is assumed that we are all salespeople, which we are when we accept the point of view that, as earnest men and women, we are constantly seeking that others should do what we would have them do, to think as we would have them think, and to feel as we would have them feel.

Of course, if we are in the position where we do not want others to do things for us, or think for us, or to feel for us, then we are hermits, and, unfortunately, there are too many hermits. So many that live up in the cloudy chimeras of their own foggy imaginations.

Let us analyse these aims. It is not very difficult to get things done for us. Very often money buys acquiescence. For instance, if we present a shilling to an outfitter, he is only too willing to give you a collar for it. Let us go a step further though, and ask what makes you present the shilling, because you are not bound to go to that particular outfitter.

It may be, of course, that you needed a collar, and you called in at the first outfitters. If so, all that happened was that the window, as you passed by, conveyed a sensation through your eye to your brain, which connected with the want of a collar, and you acted on the thought. So, you see, in that sale there was involved a little thinking.

Let us suppose, however, that you did not buy that collar at the first outfitters you saw, but rather passed a dozen on the way to a special shop where you made your purchase.

What made you pass other shops for this one? Obviously, something more than thought entered this transaction, for memory is involved. You could only know of the special shop through some kind of previous experience. You may have read an advertisement which attracted you, or you may have been recommended to go there by a friend, or you may have shopped there before, or you may have seen the window and remembered it. Whatever it was that made you go to this shop specially was something different to the instance quoted in the first place.

Actually, what would make you act under the second circumstance would be a pleasurable feeling, and there you have the secret of sales psychology.

The aim of the true sales psychologist is to induce that state of pleasurable feeling which leads to favourable action.

So the aim is not so much to make people think as to make them feel.

It you will analyse selling as you understand it, and the best way to do that is to analyse the reason why you buy things, you will find that there nearly always enters into everything that you buy, and certainly always into all important purchases, a feeling of pleasure, either for self or for the purpose of giving pleasure to others.

Since we know, too, that the memory more faithfully records that which pleases us, than that which displeases us, you can see why the whole art of sales psychology is rightly directed in the objective of pleasing.

So the objective of Sales Psychology is to please.

The standard, therefore, to be aimed at in all selling is to please permanently, and that is why the customer's attitude of mind is so important, because if you do not please her you do not make a friend. That is why it is true that the customer is "always right," even though she is not.

So the true measure of every act of the person or the business is to ask just this one question: "Will this please the customer permanently?"

Note the word "permanently." Some things do please the customers at first, but not in the long run, and it is permanent pleasure which builds business.

So everything that the customer sees, hears, tastes, touches or smells, must please, since the five senses are the gateways to the mind.

All except the cranks appreciate beauty more than ugliness, harmony more than discord, smoothness more than roughness, that which pleases the palate rather than that which does not, and aromas are preferable to stenches.

Yet businesses will use ugly advertisements, and people will use ugly voices, with an ugly manner. Travellers will present samples worn and spotty. I have more than once heard a miniature revolution going on in a store between members of a staff in the presence of customers; perhaps you have, too.

I have looked at window displays which offended all the canons of taste, just as I have known businesses which, like people, have not been started rightly, because they broke the first rule of business—to please.

So very simple, you say, and so it is, and yet why raucous voices, ill-timed letters, ugly sneers because "I would like to see something not so expensive," bawling voices over the telephone, sour looks at a troublesome request, a favour received with a grunt, ingratitude for kindness, attack instead of co-operation, and so much failure instead of success?

All because these things do not please.

You may say, "Well, anyway, I am not selling." But you are. You are selling your-self, if nothing else. If you would succeed, and the more you would succeed, the more you must please permanently.

No one stands alone in the world. You may feel as independent as you like, but you are dependent on others for your success, since success can only be measured in due relation to the way in which others will think, feel and act, as you direct them so to do.

We know through psychology that the easiest path to success is through pleasing people permanently.

I have known people, armed with no greater thought than this one of pleasing their clients or customers, go forth and win fame and fortune.

But beware, don't aim at temporary pleasing. It is easy to tickle the palate of the crowd, to win their applause temporarily, but to win it permanently is another matter.

It is easy to win a customer, for instance, with a cut price, but you do not win permanent pleasure that way.

It is easy to criticise, but not to construct. It is easy to knock, and not so easy to boost.

The easiest way is not always the surest way to build permanent sales.

There must be rules, then, that will help us to please permanently, and so there are, dug out for us by able and eminent psychologists who have dissected the human mind for us.

As you will have gathered, from what you have read, you need to form a link of memory between you and your customer or client, and that link to secure right results must be one of pleasurable memory.

You have grasped, I am sure, that that link is forged through anything that builds Confidence in the buyer's mind.

All great things of this earth are built on trust or confidence. People must believe that your services or goods are better than they can get somewhere else, either in price with quality and service equal, or that the quality is higher with price and service equal, or that the service must be higher with quality and price equal. These are the reasons why people buy.

In offering what you have for sale, you have to decide in which one of the three departments of business building you excel. Whether it is in

1. Price

or

2. Quality

or

3. Service.

It is unlikely that it will excel in all three departments, though many businesses think they do, when they excel in none really.

Actually, all successful businesses make their strong appeal on one of these three divisions.

Whichever is your strong division, either with self or the business, push it, and push it hard, and then endeavour to "step up" the other divisions.

So every individual, as well as every business, should specialise in one of the three magnets for success building.

Remember, all things being equal, the lowest price wins in the long run.

Remember, all things being equal, the highest quality wins in the long run.

Remember, all things being equal, the best service wins in the long run.

Remember, too, that business first evolved on the foundation of price.

The next stage of business was the development of quality, but the modern evolution of business is to increase the SERVICE rendering power of the organisation.

It is assumed in most businesses that prices and quality are standard, and so they are with a large number of different types of industries and businesses.

The more educated the people become, the more they realise that price alone does not matter, that "the quality of goods is remembered long after the price is forgotten."

So far has this thought been developed that even those businesses that sell on price, stress the value they give for the price, and the service that goes with the article offered for sale.

So it would seem that we must use efficiency methods to reduce the price of the article as much as possible, and then find the quality points of the article offered and stress those, and then think out better ways of service.

So far has this idea been developed that

organisations selling speciality articles maintain a large staff to see that their goods are used to the highest possible degree of efficiency. These are the people who use the slogan "Service after Purchase."

The value of understanding these main principles makes for success in business, and enables you, the student, to apply these principles to the buyers of what you have to sell.

Since human nature varies, and since the article you sell may be applied to the user in so many ways, you, in exercising your initiative, can adapt your service to the user much better when you understand the principle than if you only know a few details.

For instance, let us take this principle of salesmanship. We know through psychology that over 80% of people fire eye-minded, so no matter what you sell, 80% of sales-matter or talk should be through appeal to the eye.

In other words, we are appearance-minded. Looks count for 80% at least, and the more immature the mind, the more looks count. This one principle applied in selling makes sales easier.

Your fertile mind can immediately imagine all sorts of ways that you can adapt when you sell through the eye.

The next psychological principle to remember is that 80% of people are influenced more through their feelings than through their intellect. Human nature stories of interest and romance appeal more than facts. If you doubt this statement, watch the crowd at a cinema looking at a romantic picture, and then at an Educational film.

So dig out the romance in what you sell, and dig out the romance in your own life. There is one always. Tell the world, tactfully, of course, but be human, alive and interesting, and make the article you sell thrill with life.

I instanced at the beginning of this chapter the incident of the collar purchase. You will note how feelings entered even into that simple purchase, as you will find it does in 80% of all that you purchase.

Let me give you the final point that will help you in selling. In getting others to agree with you, whether outside an organisation or in, you will have had the experience of presenting all the points as I have illustrated them, and yet you will have failed.

The reason is that the hardest part of salesmanship is to clinch.

The secret is this: Give the buyer a choice of two things, either choice involving the decision you are seeking. Here are some practical instances.

Don't say, "Coming for a walk?" Say, "Where shall we walk to, the river or to the Park?"

Don't say, "May we take your order?" Say, "Shall I send these or those?"

Don't say, "Shall I call next week?" Say, "Shall I call Monday or Tuesday?"

Over the telephone don't say, "Can I come and see you?" Say, "I would like to see you, would you rather I came this afternoon or tomorrow morning?"

If you are selling typewriters, don't say "What about it?" as I once heard an intelligent salesman say; rather say, "What colour ribbon would you prefer?"

This idea of choice can be used in letters as well as in conversations. There are times when it can be used in advertisements, but I want you now to make this idea of choice a mental habit, so that when you are making a request you will use the "choice" idea automatically.

So, as you can gather, salesmanship is no longer a haphazard affair. It is one of the new arts of the day, and as you master these principles given in this book, so will you find your position in life made more successful, easier, happier and more comforting.

CHAPTER TEN

THE IMPORTANCE OF PUBLIC SPEAKING

AS I have said in my book, "The Master Public Speaker," the power is with the speaker. Talkers get the most pay.

In order to make Staff Training effective, there is no doubt as to the value of being able to express your ideas on your feet.

In every industry I have had anything to do with, I know at least one employer who has made himself an effective public speaker for life through Staff Training.

Feeling the urge for getting closer in touch with his staff, he has taken these ideas, and extracted points from them and linked them up with other points of his own experience, and gradually equipped himself to speak on his feet, by holding weekly meetings of his staff, and talking to them as well as he could, gradually becoming more proficient as he went along.

So there's the first lesson in Public Speaking.

START.

If you do not wish to start speaking extempore, and you would not be wise to attempt to do so unless you have had previous experience, then commence by reading a paper, and read one as often as you can get anyone to listen to you.

One day, when the occasion is perhaps not so important, you could speak from your paper. That is, you could underline the most important statements and then talk around them.

Later on, you could speak from a number of headlines, and as you acquire expertness you could do with less and less notes.

If you get enough practise, the time comes when you can speak without any notes at all, particularly if you use the method of Initialisation as outlined in a previous book.

Whenever you are at a public meeting get up and ask a question. If you are nervous about it, write it down and then read it out This accustoms you to the sound of your own voice.

THE BEST EXERCISE

The best exercise for the public speaker is reading aloud, standing up.

You need to become used to the sound of your own voice, and accustomed to it, standing up, so read aloud every day for five minutes. If you can, do this. Pin up on the wall something you would like to memorise or know about, any article, say, from your favourite trade paper, and while you are lathering your face in the morning, read aloud. You thus get information and practise at the same time, for most men are allowed to make noises in the bath room, which would not be allowed elsewhere, and reading aloud is more tolerable than singing.

TIPS ON POISE

The poise of the public speaker is important. There is a dignity in stance, typified by Lord Davidson, the late Archbishop of Canterbury, Bramwell Booth, the late Lord Curzon, and Horatio Bottomley, which helps the speaker make the right start.

Study these tips:

1. Stand up straight, in the boxer's attitude (as far as the feet are concerned, of course), chest up, chin up a little, and feel you are king of the world, even though your knees want to quake.
2. Don't lean over the table, and don't tidy it up. It is tidy, anyway, and your fidgetting only annoys the audience.
3. Don't sway backwards and forwards on your feet (hence the boxer's attitude). One prominent politician ruined his career because of this unfortunate habit, for as soon as he got into his stride, and was

well away with his sway, his opponents commenced singing "Rock-a-bye baby," keeping tune with his sway.

4. Beware of mannerisms such as fiddling with your money, or your watch chain, or a button, or trying to poke your finger through the palm of the other hand. Get a friend to tell you of any mannerisms which detract from your speaking. Your wife generally makes your best critic, for she is as anxious as you are for your success.
5. Beware of over gesture. Far better to make none at all than to make too many. The best tip I know on this point is to tie your hands behind your back with cotton until you forget you have the cotton there at all. If this is not practicable keep your hands behind your back until you forget you have any.
6. Learn to take in all parts of your audience. A man will more likely believe what you say if you can look him in the eye now and again, so plan to look at all the eyes of the audience, and have everyone seated so that they can see you. Beware of the people who sit behind you. They will never believe you have made a good speech.
7. Speak to the last man in the last row.

Many speakers plan to have a friend in the back row, and they "tick-tack "back to the speaker, whether his voice is dropping at the end of sentences, whether he is going too quickly, or whether he can be heard at all. At some meetings the last rows are under a balcony, and it is very difficult to make the voice carry into the small, confined space there.

HOW TO CONSTRUCT A SPEECH

The man who attempts to construct a speech during the Chairman's introduction, as I once saw a noble Lord attempt to do is as effectually courting disaster as this peer of the realm rightly deserved and received.

Preparation for the construction of speeches should go on all the time. You must begin to acquire raw material at once.

The best plan and the simplest is this: Procure 26 envelopes, size 8" x 11", and letter them "A" to "Z "on the left-hand side. Then on the right put the headings of the articles so filed. For instance, under "S" you could write on the right-hand side, "Scenes in the House of Commons," if that is the heading of the article.

You should collect stories, and if you wish, cross index them. One man I know in London has 9,000 cards indexed, and his stories are the talk of his friends.

In this way you can gather points which lend to your speeches authority and acceptance, and you will pass as a man of capacity. With this reservoir of matter to draw upon, what to do with it is the next question.

If you will arrange the points under the following headings you will find that it is comparatively easy to construct a speech in a short space of time.

For instance, on the left write:—

INTRODUCTION : Here write a pointer which will interest the audience immediately, or tell a story about them and you, if you can. (You will find many stories can be changed to fit the occasion.)

STATEMENT OF AIM : Here tell the audience what is your aim. Tell them what it is you wish to have them believe or think. Be tactful in your presentation. Don't say, "I want you to spend ten pounds with me," but rather, "I want to tell you the interesting story of the growth of this Movement, and how you can take part in it."

REASONS FOR YOUR SPEECH AND AIM : Every speech has an aim. There ought to be a reason for it and for your aim. There are a series of arguments which you can bring forward, and you can arrange these pointers, proceeding from what the audience will believe to what you want them to believe. This is called proceeding from the known to the unknown, or from the common to the uncommon, which all bright barristers use.

PROOF OF REASONS : You should never assert without proving the facts. Prove your points up to the hilt. Prove by print and authority, and, if possible, appeal to the eye. You will remember what we said in the previous books about the importance of appealing to the eye.

APPEAL TO THE EMOTIONS : In every speech there is an opportunity for an appeal to an emotion. You can appeal to the audience's feelings of:

Courage,

Faith,

Enthusiasm,

Loyalty,

Optimism,

Hopefulness,

Pride,

Duty,

Kindness,

Fairness,

Ambition,

Service,

or

Joy.

Always use one or more of these emotions or feelings in every speech.

PERORATION : This should knit together all parts of the speech. You should give a short resume of the main points and always ask the audience to do something definitely. Have them promise you something. Make them even sing, as the audience did I addressed this morning, when everyone got up and sang "Pack up your troubles in your old kit bag and SMILE." Or it may be you meant them to sign a form, or actually do something there and then. Anyway, close the meeting with some central objective for them to carry away and perform. This makes your speech successful.

HOW TO HANDLE YOUR AUDIENCE

Handling an audience is easier than one expects. Sometimes the audience is as shy as the speaker, although the latter should lose his shyness first.

One of the ways which helps the embryo speaker is to practise deep breathing, and as he starts speaking he should do a little then, for this gives poise and confidence.

Another way that helps in handling an audience is to stand a little above them. Few take any notice of speakers on their own level. All the big crowds in Hyde Park are around the speakers perched up on high. If necessary, use a box to stand on whenever the audience is over fifty.

ALWAYS LOOK THE AUDIENCE IN THE EYE. All beginners fail to do this, yet this is essential if you would capture the crowd.

You can start a little diffidently, if you like, which is better than commencing too confidently. In any case, be sure to end confidently, because no one takes you more at your own valuation than an audience.

Be sure NOT to start with an apology. If you do, the audience will see that defect in everything that you say. Don't even tell them you have a cold, because they will think you cannot think straightly.

Introduce a little humour, but not too much. Be sure to get the audience to laugh with you, and not at you. Don't make jokes at your own expense, otherwise you are likely to be taken seriously.

Don't talk too long. Most speeches are too long, anyway. An after-dinner speech should not last more than eight minutes, and ten to twenty minutes is the utmost limit for talking to staffs, and ten-minute talks are more effective.

MASS PSYCHOLOGY

One of the reasons why staff training is so successful is that under the more able experts the members of the staff are not only instructed individually, but also in the mass.

It is well-known that the various states of mind, such as loyalty, the team spirit, and the crowd spirit, can only be induced by mass meetings. Just as these meetings can be so successful, so can they be disastrous.

For that reason I always counsel executives to start public speaking in this way, if they have not done public speaking before.

Get together ten to twenty of the executive, who are in the main loyal to you already, and commence talking to them, and keep at it at least once a fortnight until you are more proficient than you expected. It is time then to go to the main mass of your staff, and you will find that the previous training that you will have had will stand you in great stead when you are dealing with the larger body.

After you have gathered confidence and feel that you can handle the situation, ask for questions, and say as one executive did, "No one will get the sack for what he says in this room," and you will probably have illuminating replies. Some will hurt, but a hurt that festers inside the mind poisons the whole work of that particular individual, and it is better to have it out, so the mass meeting performs a useful psychological surgical operation.

You will begin to get ideas. You will find a ready flow of suggestions. You will find that the suggestion box will be used more frequently.

You will find that workers will take a keener interest. At a place where these meetings were held a new extension was recently added, and it was announced at one of these meetings that a tour of inspection would take place on Saturday at 12.5 (the works closed at 12).

Every member of over 200 of the staff queued up—not one was missing, and so an impromptu meeting was held there and then.. It was one of the most amazing meetings held, for a few words would be said by the speaker standing of times on a machine, and his discourse continued on another, until the whole of the new building had been canvassed in this way.

It was pronounced one of the most successful meetings held, particularly as there grew out of this meeting the idea that each worker should be held responsible for a section of the new place, in an endeavour to keep the place as spotless as it was then.

ADVANTAGES OF STAFF MEETINGS

There is no doubt that, by this method of speaking, labour turnover is reduced, profits are increased, wages are higher, and the standard of output is very high, because of the increased interest of the worker.

Speaking as a business counsel, I do not mind stating that some of the best ideas I give firms are partly suggested by workers whose enthusiasm has not been hitherto tapped. Few workers bring their brains to work, and fewer their heart, and that is what staff meetings will do; they do unite HEAD POWER, HEART POWER and HAND POWER. It should be seen that all such suggestions received are suitably rewarded.

A FINAL SUGGESTION

If you are thinking of starting these meetings, it is useful to see that a little refreshment is provided No meeting is so dry then.

Also remember that you will need every ounce

of persistency and courage, for few will support you at the beginning, and you will be tempted at many to give it up, but carry on, until you will find someone arising in your midst who can carry on the job of Club Leader and leave you free for the next big job of business building.

That this idea is valuable, may I conclude again by giving you my experience?

CASE "A." A firm increased sales 25%.

CASE "B." A firm increased sales 22%.

CASE "C." A small firm increased sales 100%.

CASE "D." A medium firm increased sales 68%.

CASE "E." A firm, the largest of its kind in the Midlands, reports an increase of 55% in two years.

CASE "F." A firm reports a 19% increase in sales.

CASE "G." A firm reports an increase of 38%.

And there are four other firms who report increases from 18%.

Please note that the smallest increase

reported in last year's staff training was 18%. This should give encouragement to you in your endeavours to increase the happiness and prosperity of your business.